Twin Flame Love:

How to Reunite with Your Other Half Through Meditation, Telepathy, and the Law of Attraction

Beratla Kasovich

Table of Contents

Introduction

Before we get started, I would like to thank and congratulate you for downloading your copy of *Twin Flame Love: How to Reunite with Your Other Half Through Meditation, Telepathy, and The Law of Attraction*. By reading this book, you are answering the call of your soul to find your twin flame and undergo the deep healing that this intense and passionate connection brings.

The concept of the twin flame is by no means new, but it has come into the mainstream focus in a big way in the modern age. Psychics and spiritual healers theorize that this is due to the high amount of spiritual energy and the ascendance of consciousness that is taking place with those of us on Earth today. While in ancient times a twin flame connection was a very rare occurrence, scores of people have been experiencing the reunion with their twins in the time of the New Age. This mass reunion brings a flood of light energy to the planet in one of its darkest times, and many teachers are offering guidance to help others find and reunite with their twins to bring even more of this potent healing energy to the world.

It is my hope that by absorbing the information in this book, you, too, will be able to reunite with your twin and unlock the world of love that is waiting especially for you. The journey to find and connect with your twin is one of the most profound and difficult, but the rewards you will both reap are worth the effort a thousand times over. If you are ready to undertake this incredible journey, then let's begin.

Chapter 1

Understanding the Role that Your Twin Flame Plays in Your Life

The concepts of soulmates and twin flames have been around for thousands of years, dating back at least to the time of ancient Greece. The great philosopher Plato may have originated the concept when he theorized that there was a time when humans were so great, the gods had to split them in two to ensure that we would not grow to overpower them. Many credit this as the beginning of the notion that souls can be two halves of the same whole, though it is widely accepted today that the two souls comprising the twin flame unit are full and complete unto themselves.

If you pay close attention to literature throughout the centuries, you will find that different authors hinted at the concept of twin flames in their writing. In "Sonnet 116," infamous master of love William Shakespeare writes:

> *"...Love is not love*
> *Which alters when it alteration finds.*

Or bends with the remover to remove:

O, no! it is an ever-fixed mark,

That looks on tempests and is not shaken;

It is the star to every wandering bark,

...

Love alters not with his brief hours and weeks,

But bears it out even to the edge of doom,

If this be error, and upon me proved,

I never writ, nor no man ever loved."

This sonnet hints at the eternal and unconditional nature of twin flame love, which provides a template for us to learn what it truly means to accept and love another human being without judgment or reservation.

In the classic novel *Wuthering Heights* by Emily Bronte, heroine Catherine speaks of her twin flame, Heathcliff, in no uncertain terms:

> *"My great miseries in this world have been Heathcliff's miseries, and I watched and felt each from the beginning: my great thought in living is himself. If all else perished, and he remained, I should still continue to be; and if all else remained, and he were annihilated, the universe would turn to a mighty stranger: I should not seem a part of it. —My love for Linton is like the foliage in the woods: time will change it, I'm well aware, as winter changes the trees. My love for Heathcliff resembles the eternal rocks beneath:*

a source of little visible delight, but necessary. Nelly, I am Heathcliff! He's always, always in my mind: not as a pleasure, any more than I am always a pleasure to myself, but as my own being. So don't talk of our separation again..." (Ch.9)

While today's psychologists would insist that this is an unhealthy relationship, the twin flame connection truly is this closely interwoven. Lines become blurred and, for the unprepared twins, individual identities can become tangled and lost as the two become swept away by the tide of divine oneness.

So, what exactly is a twin flame? Let's take a closer look.

What is a Twin Flame?

To put it simply, twin flames are soul mirrors. They reflect the deepest truths of ourselves back to us so that we can grow, learn, and heal. Twin flames are two complete souls that form one unit when reunited, though this reunion is not an easy thing to achieve.

When they are split, twin flames each go their separate ways, learning and experiencing all that they can on Earth. They only very rarely meet in person throughout the centuries as they each have their own important lessons to learn. Sometimes they take turns incarnating, with one living a physical life and the other watching over them and providing guidance from the other side of the veil. Yet there is always this feeling of missing someone, of searching for something that is perhaps undefined for the separated twin flame.

It is not until both souls have reached maturity that twin flames begin to cross one another's paths again. Although a certain stage of soul evolution must have been reached before twins start seeing each other on the physical plane, this does not mean that both are ready to reunite. The twin flame connection is intense beyond imagining, and the passion and intense love that comes with it can be overwhelming for the unprepared.

Twin flames do not begin to cross paths in the physical world until they are nearing their final incarnations. They will need the wisdom of hundreds of lifetimes and thousands of lessons learned to handle the challenge of being together. Although twin flame relationships are not always romantic in nature, the overwhelming majority of them are due to the intense passion that marks their bonds to one another. They do not need to be heterosexual relationships to be a twin flame relationship, but the yin and yang aspects of this connection will manifest in other ways.

It is said that twin flames reunite in their very last incarnations so that they can reach enlightenment and ascend together. Their reunion not only plays a huge role in their own spiritual growth, but it contributes to the ascension of the planet as a whole. We will see more on this in a minute.

Twin flame relationships are marked by deep psychic and telepathic bonds and a mirroring of life circumstances. Because your twin flame is meant to reflect you back to yourself, you may find many synchronicities between what they have experienced and what you have experienced. The time that your twin flame arrives in your life will be marked by great change, as they have potent lessons to teach you and to learn themselves.

Another hallmark of twin flame relationships is extreme emotional intensity. The emotional highs and lows experienced by the two people in a twin flame relationship are more drastic than those in any other relationship. Because the energy of the twin flame connection is so large, it opens the chakras wider than ever, allowing the individuals to release and process more of their emotions, memories, and old baggage. This high emotional intensity will change how twins understand themselves as individuals, and the shift in personal identity can be more than unprepared twins can handle.

Nonetheless, when your twin flame comes into your life, there is an unmistakable sense of familiarity, as though you've known this person before. When you are with your twin flame, there is a remarkable sense of "coming home." Indeed, you may even feel a sense of looking into your own soul when you look into the eyes of your twin, for you are two souls born of the same source. In essence, you *are* your twin flame, and your twin flame is you.

How is a Twin Flame Different from a Soulmate?

The short answer to the difference between a twin flame and a soulmate is that, while you can have many soulmates, you only have one twin. Soulmates are a group of souls who travel together throughout various incarnations, also known as a soul family. Soulmates can be friends, family members, lovers, teachers, healers, and even enemies, yet each has an important lesson to teach us when they come into our lives.

Every soulmate connection that you experience leading up to your reunion with your twin flame is meant to teach and prepare you for this encounter. Their lessons can be pleasant, painful, difficult, or complex, but all go towards the same end—bringing you the healing that you need to be ready for the bigger challenge of reuniting with your twin.

As soulmates, our groups are cut from the same spiritual cloth, so to speak. Although not all soulmates incarnate at the same time, they are never far from one another. We run into our soulmates more often than we may realize, as we bump up against one another or cross paths only briefly to give an important lesson.

While some soulmates may stay with us for our entire lives, others may only stick around for a few months or years, leaving when the wisdom they have to teach us has been passed on. Then there are those whose presence in our lives is fleeting as they pop in for a brief moment to give us some encouragement, a piece of advice, or a challenging lesson that we must push through on our own.

Though you will not see your twin flame in every incarnation on Earth, you will always have soulmates close at hand to guide and support you, and you, them. These soul kins are one of the many blessings we experience in life, but although their companionship is sweet, they can never satiate the eternal longing we have to be reunited with our twins.

How to Recognize Your Twin Flame

It takes great spiritual openness and awareness to recognize your twin flame the first time you see them. This level of spiritual enlightenment takes a fair bit of practice. We'll go into more detail on this subject later in the book.

However, even the untrained or unprepared seeker will marvel at the sense of familiarity and recognition that come with the first encounter with one's twin flame. You feel instantly at ease with this person, as though you can be your full self without reservation. Conversation comes easily, and you feel you can tell them anything without being judged.

Long after you have parted ways, you will find your thoughts returning to this person. You will inexplicably miss them, and wonder how you can miss someone you have just met for the first time. You might stare a little too hard, or hold your bodies a little too close, unable to resist the magnetic pull between you.

There's a good chance that one or both of you will be unavailable, perhaps married or in stable, committed relationships. Perhaps you have career concerns keeping you apart or live in locations very far from one another. Twin flame reunions are marked with a certain level of chaos and disruption. You'll find that you have to crack the world somewhat to make room for you to be together. We'll look closer at why this would be the case in the next chapter.

The Roles that Our Twin Flames Play

As we saw earlier, twin flames are mirror souls. You will recognize your twin by finding someone whose experiences and personality traits mirror your own, either in the positive or the negative. Twin flame pairs are a perfectly matched set of yin and yang energy. Your differences will be the perfect opposite of one another. This gives you the opportunity to see what kind of person you want to be, what kind of person you don't want to be, and areas where you can improve. For example, if you are withdrawn and grumpy, your twin will be outgoing and cheerful. The opposition that your twin presents to you will give you an opportunity to grow and learn.

A hallmark trait of the twin flame relationship is the lack of judgment between the two. A reunited pair of twin flames will love and accept each other unconditionally, which teaches these highest of virtues through the highest of relationship models. You have no choice but to love your twin flame through thick and thin. This is often a very scary experience due to the unprecedented level of vulnerability you will feel with this person.

The purpose of the twin flame relationship is to challenge souls to evolve and grow. The time that your twin enters your life will mark a great spiritual awakening within you both. Your spiritual growth will be accelerated at a lightning pace, which can be overwhelming to those who are unprepared. This explosion of growth comes not only from the intensity of love and passion you feel from one another but from the challenges you will each face when you meet this energy. Are you prepared to accept this kind of love? Are you prepared to give it? Can you handle this radical vulnerability, or will the challenge be too much for you to face?

The lessons your twin flame will pose to you go much deeper than your development as an individual in this incarnation. Twin flame bonds last for all eternity, and their work pertains to missions that happen on a soul level. As lightworkers, twin flames share a unique mission to bring more spiritual energy to the third dimension, to help those on Earth to raise their vibrations and ascend to the next level of consciousness.

The work you do to reunite with your twin unlocks knowledge of soul lessons and stores it in the collective unconscious, where it can be accessed by the others. As you and your twin flame move ever closer to one another, your souls move a vast amount of energy to clear an open path for you. This movement breaks patterns of energetic stagnation and aids in the forward progression of humanity's ascension. Once reunited, your complete bond unleashes a tide of light energy that washes over the planet and all who inhabit it. We need this light energy now to combat the negativity running rampant in the world today.

So, as you can see, the role of twin flames extends far beyond personal growth and development. Your happiness will be the key to generating the potential for more happiness in the world around you. Yet this achievement comes with a lot of work, for the lessons learned at this high soul level require advanced wisdom and spiritual evolution to attain. This is something that you can do with proper dedication and focus. Do not be afraid to answer the call of your soul's mission, but give yourself to it fully and you will find all the guidance and aid you need to achieve your purpose.

A twin flame relationship goes much farther beyond your typical *Romeo and Juliet* romance story than some may have led you to believe. However, this bond holds the potential for tremendous healing, and the journey will unlock powers within you that go much deeper than your ability to fall in love.

Chapter 2

Why Your Twin Flame May Not Be Ready to Reunite

If you've been searching for your twin flame for some time with no success, there's a good chance that your twin may not be ready to reunite with you. Even if you have crossed paths, you might not have recognized one another because one or both of you weren't ready to face the confrontation.

The main reason for this unpreparedness is a lack of sufficient spiritual evolution. Because the twin flame relationship is so demanding, you will not be equipped to meet the challenges you will both face. When your individual energies are not strong enough to withstand the enormous force of your reunion, you will resist the magnetic pull of your twin until you are ready.

Facing your twin unprepared could have dire consequences for your relationship. Should you meet too soon, you could kick up a storm of bad karma and spiritual baggage that you will have to sort through to be together again.

Depending on how badly you hurt one another in your unprepared states, you could force yourselves apart again for several more lifetimes, then have to heal that pain on top of everything else you already have to work through.

Fortunately, you have the benefit of finding the knowledge that you need to prepare yourself now. When you know what signs to look for to discover which parts of you and your twin are not ready to reunite, then you can consciously work on healing yourself and sending healing to your twin.

The 8 Stages of Twin Flame Reunion

Understanding the twin flame reunion process can give you an upper hand in successfully finding and reuniting with your twin. Although each twin flame reunion is unique unto itself, the process tends to follow a distinguishable set of stages. It helps a lot to know which stage you and your twin are in. You may have even met and had a relationship with this person before without knowing they were your twin flame. If so, these signs may clue you into the true nature of your connection.

The Longing

The first stage of twin flame reunion is marked by an intense longing for one another. From the moment you are first separated, you and your twin will always feel a sense of abstract longing for some unknown source of fulfillment throughout all your incarnations. You'll feel as though something is missing, and you will search for different means of fulfillment according to your distinct personalities, times of incarnation, and the options available to you.

Yet as you come ever closer to one another through the spiritual growth you are both undertaking, your longing will begin to solidify into a sense of desire for your "other half." You'll know that what you are looking for is a sense of fulfillment through relationship. You may even become conscious, as you are now, that what you are seeking is your twin flame.

Both twins will need to feel this longing on some level before you will have a chance of crossing one another's paths. The stronger your desire to meet each other, the faster you will alter the courses of your paths to find one another. Meeting and reuniting with your twin flame is your ultimate destiny—the true question is whether you are ready to meet your fate.

Orbits Approaching

Your intense desire to meet your twin flame will inevitably bring you closer and closer together. As your orbits approach and prepare to cross paths, you will feel this sense of impending destiny. You may feel it as a warning, a blessing, or an abstract energetic door that you are about to walk through. Your unconscious will respond based on whatever baggage you have beneath the surface, so you may feel a sense of fear, anticipation, exhilaration, or restlessness.

The time leading up to the meeting of two twin flames is marked by synchronicity and spirit signs. Fateful encounters with people and animals, repeating numbers, words, and names can all be signs that your meeting with your twin flame is approaching.

The Meeting

After the great energetic buildup, the two twin flames finally meet. Fate will have led them through a series of steps, coincidences, and intuitive signposts to find one another in the world.

The moment of the meeting will be intense, and if they are open, both twins will feel the impact of their meeting like a shockwave through their bodies. The memory of this meeting will be stamped on their minds, and they will continue to think of the other long after the initial encounter has passed.

The Destruction

When two twin flames meet in person, they may find each other at an inopportune time. One or both may be in committed relationships, they may live in different regions of the world, or they may have career constraints that make immediate union difficult. These obstacles mark the beginning of the destruction that twin flame reunions bring.

One major purpose for twin flame reunions is their ability to move massive amounts of energy as they reach for one another. These obstacles not only test to see if they are truly ready to come back together and to prepare them for the greater obstacles ahead in the relationship, but they also force them to tear down old structures and open the door to allow new energy into their lives. These energetic doors open the way for new energy to come into the world as well, so the destruction serves more than the two twins involved in the reunion.

Initial Bliss

Once the dust has settled from whatever destruction arising out of their meeting, the twin flames are free to enjoy the sweet bliss that comes from their reunion. This phase is marked by immense passion and a honeymoon phase like no other. The energy surrounding the reunited twin flames is so strong it will be tangible to those who encounter them together. People remark on how natural they seem together, as though they have been together forever.

Reunited twins may be able to feel the energetic pulse of their connection through physical intimacy. Every kiss seems to linger on the lips for hours after they have parted—if it is even possible for them to leave one another while in the bliss phase. Lovemaking will seem otherworldly as potent energy awakens dormant kundalini energy. This interchange of energy provides a catalyst for accelerated spiritual awakening and a great change to happen within and around the reunited twins.

Reality Hits

As the initial bliss phase begins to pass, the twins are hit with the reality of having to work through their relationship dynamics. Even the most otherworldly connection will still face the trials of mundane reality. These trials will seem more intense, however, as the twins must cope with the extreme energy that their connection creates.

Their yin and yang aspects will naturally clash with one another, which is the catalyst for great growth between the two—if they can rise to meet the challenge. On top of all that, the amplified emotions that a twin flame connection brings will further complicate the situation for the two. This phase following the initial bliss phase can create the waves of the "extreme highs and extreme lows" dynamic that is a hallmark of twin flame connections.

The Runner and the Chaser

Should it be the case that one twin is less spiritually evolved than the other, which is very common, the twins will likely act out the runner and the chaser stage. The less evolved of the two will find themselves quickly overwhelmed by the intensity of the connection and seek to run away from it, unable to handle the higher level of relationship that is now required of them.

The more spiritually evolved person in the relationship will likely take on the role of the chaser, constantly seeking to forgive and make amends in order to make the relationship work. The runner may choose to separate physically from the chaser, either by leaving or breaking off the relationship, though they may also run within the constraints of the relationship by becoming aloof and unresponsive.

This runner and chaser dynamic is responsible for the messiness of twin flame relationships. The two can break up and come back together several times, sometimes even after separating for several years. Onlookers will wonder what on Earth is going on with the two as their relationship begins to resemble something from a television drama.

The most unprepared twins may end up leaving their relationship in this phase in their current lifetimes. The separation that can come from the runner and chaser phase may prove to be permanent. Should this be the case, they'll have to start all over again in their next incarnations. However, those who successfully work through their differences and find healthy ways to cope with the high emotional intensity of their connection will move on to the final stage of twin flame reunion.

Reunion as a Baptism by Fire

The moment of your true reunion and full commitment to one another will be the most profound and important moment of your relationship because it is the moment that you both say "yes." When both parties have stopped running and chasing each other and decided to embrace the connection between their souls, the "yes" comes from the deepest level of their souls. Such an affirmation of the soul will unlock even more spiritual growth, and the twins will be firmly on the path of spiritual enlightenment.

Signs that Your Twin Isn't Ready

Because you won't know whether your twin is ready to reunite with you if you haven't met them yet, it's important to look for other signs to indicate whether this might be the case. If you have a past relationship or an on-again, off-again relationship with someone that matches the stages listed above, this may be when you realize that this person is your twin flame and you are stuck in the runner-chaser phase of your reunion. However, you must use your intuition to distinguish whether this is truly a higher spiritual connection or simply a dysfunctional relationship. Whatever the case, you can determine whether your twin flame is ready to reunite with you or not by some of the following signs:

You have been consciously searching for your twin flame for some time with no success. If you are spiritually evolved enough to be seeking the twin flame relationship and have not had even an inkling of who your twin might be or whether they are currently incarnated with you, the chances are that you may be more ready for the meeting than your twin is.

You are highly intuitive but cannot pick up on the energy of your twin flame. This is likely a sign that their signal is too weak for you to find. Your twin will need to evolve more spiritually to strengthen their energy and put themselves on the path to reuniting with you.

It may also be the case that they did not incarnate with you in this lifetime, but because they will be acting as a guide for you on the other side, you will likely pick up on their energy all around you. If you have a feeling that someone specific is always watching you and this energy does not belong to a loved one who has passed from your current lifetime, chances are that this is your twin flame in spirit form.

You have met someone whom you had a tremendous connection with, but before the relationship even got off the ground, they inexplicably vanished. This may have been your twin flame running away from the intensity of your connection because they were not ready to handle it.

Signs that You Are Not Ready

Holding the mirror up to oneself can be a hard thing to master. However, if you truly want to find your twin flame, you must be prepared to do the deep soul-work that is necessary for your reunion. Here are some signs that you might not be ready to meet your twin flame:

You have a lot of trouble coping with your own emotions.

You are a highly confrontational person and get swept up in a lot of little ego dramas.

You have just begun on your current spiritual path, and the concept of a twin flame is very new to you.

You feel victimized or martyred a lot of the time.

You are stuck in the past with a previous relationship and are holding onto your baggage so tight that it prevents you from moving forward in your life.

You have met someone that you felt an enormous draw to, but you cut off the connection because you felt scared or overwhelmed by this person (assuming that the person was healthy).

What Do I Need to Do to Be Ready for My Twin?

The best thing you can do to prepare yourself for reuniting with your twin flame is to work on you. By learning to love and accept yourself completely, you will be able to open yourself to this kind of love and to give it when you are re-united with your twin.

You must also be willing to dig deep and remove energetic and emotional blockages that will keep you from opening the path to your twin flame. Shadow work and energy work are great ways to look in the mirror and be in touch with the parts of you that need the most healing.

Can I Help My Twin Heal and Be Ready to Reunite?

The short answer to this question is: yes, absolutely. To heal anyone other than yourself, you need that person's express permission to send energy; however, because your twin flame is essentially another you, the rules are slightly less rigid here. The important thing is to remember that you cannot seek to keep them from learning critical lessons that they have chosen or force them onto a path for which they are not ready.

What you *can* do is send them love and project your energy out to them so that they can pick up your trail, so to speak. You can send healing energy their way and make it available to them, but ultimately, they must choose to accept the gift and use it for their own healing. Healing your twin flame is the focus of the next chapter, so we will leave off here for now and move forward with this focus.

Chapter 3

Sending Love and Healing to Your Twin Flame

One of the most beautiful and profound things you can do on your spiritual path is to send love and healing to someone you have yet to meet. Through undertaking this selfless act (and you must be certain that your intentions are truly pure here), you will establish initial contact with your twin and introduce your energies to one another in a pure and loving way. Such a preliminary move will help pave a gentle path for your reunion and set the relationship on a positive foot from the very start.

Beginning to establish contact with your twin flame through sending love and healing is an excellent starting point because of how much you will learn about working with energy, which, as we will see in the next chapter, is the foundation for becoming proficient with telepathic communication. The skills you will learn through the exercises in this chapter will prepare you for more direct telepathic connection with your twin in the pages to come.

Intuiting the Issues

When first starting out with sending healing to your twin flame, it helps to try to intuit the issues they are dealing with. This will acquaint you with their energy and help you to develop your psychic abilities for better telepathic communication.

For this exercise, you can choose to use a doll, stuffed animal, or generic drawing of the body to represent your twin flame. Draw or attach the symbols of each of the seven major chakras (root/red, sacral or naval/orange, solar plexus/yellow, heart/green, throat/blue, third eye/indigo, crown/violet) along the spine of the body. You can also choose to use a chart of the chakras in ascending order for this exercise.

Take a few moments to clear your mind by closing your eyes and doing some deep breathing. Set your intention to connect with your twin flame and only your twin flame. If you are in touch with your spiritual guidance, you can ask to be connected with the spiritual guidance of your twin. When you feel the connection is established, open your eyes and turn your attention to the chakra representations.

Here you will be looking to see which of the chakras you are most drawn to. When you find your attention pulled to one more than the rest, make a note of which one it is. This chakra will represent the aspect of life that your twin flame needs the most assistance in healing. You can repeat the exercise as many times as you want until you feel that you have found the areas that are in most need of help.

As you do this exercise, you might find that you start receiving information about specific issues pertaining to each chakra. This could include knowledge of physical illness or injury, mental and emotional trauma, past life injuries, toxic mental and emotional patterns, and so on. Keep a journal on hand to make a note of the information you receive. It will inform your insights into the relationship after you meet.

For the next part of the exercise, make your way back into a meditative state with deep breathing. When you are ready, you will begin sending healing energy to your twin flame specific to each chakra you were drawn to during the previous step. To enhance the energy you send, you may hold an item or wear a cloth with predominant colors that match the color of the chakra you are healing. Alternatively, you can work with crystals that correspond to the appropriate chakras.

Visualize the form of your twin flame in your mind's eye. As you strengthen the established connection once more, slowly begin to surround them with light that matches the color of the chakras you were directed to, one at a time. Don't hit them with a direct beam of color, but see the color swirling around them gently as a cloud of colored light. The color is so wispy that your twin flame will be able to breathe it into their body if they choose to do so. Remember not to force any of this energy onto them—all you can do is make the energy available to them and offer it up, but they must choose whether or not to accept it.

Should you feel your twin flame refusing the energy you are offering, don't be alarmed. Twins who are in most need of healing may be so closed off that they are not ready to open up to receive the healing. Be patient and repeat this exercise a few times, gently offering the energy for them to accept. Over time, they will become more familiar with your energy and will likely begin to draw on the healing you have lovingly sent.

If you receive any additional information throughout this portion of the exercise, be sure to make a note of it in your journal for later reference. Repeat this exercise as often as you wish.

Sending Healing Through Dreams

One of the first places we learn to interact with others telepathically is in the ethereal realm of dreams. Lucid dreaming, or dreaming with conscious awareness, is one form of astral travel or traveling through the energetic planes with one's energy body. Learning how to lucid dream takes a lot of practice. The key to unlocking your ability to lucid dream is to get into the habit of asking yourself in your waking life if you are currently dreaming. As you stop and ask yourself this question in the physical world, your subconscious mind will absorb the habit, and you will start asking yourself the same question in your dreams.

While you don't need to know how to lucid dream to connect with your twin flame, it helps boost your healing abilities if you do. Whether you learn to lucid dream or not, this exercise will help you to establish contact with your twin flame in the dream realm and begin bringing messages of love and healing.

Before you go to bed, spend a few minutes in quiet meditation. Allow all stress and tension from the previous day to melt away. As your mind clears, draw your focus to connecting with the energy of your twin flame, as you did in the previous exercise.

For this first part of the exercise, you will need to prepare a message in advance for your twin flame. You must take care to keep this message very simple, to make it easier for yourself to remember and for your twin to understand. Appropriate initial contact could include messages of love and a desire to meet and reunite, or you can let them know that you are at their service. Your message should be no more than three short sentences.

In your mind's eye, visualize yourself meeting your twin flame in the ethereal world of dreams. See the moment of recognition between you as you approach, and as they open their energy and face you, gently deliver your message. See them accepting and understanding your message, then give a warm embrace, a gentle kiss, or a handshake as you feel is appropriate, and return to your body.

As you hold your conscious awareness in your body, set an intention to travel to your twin flame that night in your dreams. Speak the following words aloud, or repeat them firmly in your head: "Tonight when I fall asleep, I will travel to find my twin flame, and only my twin flame, to deliver a message of love and healing." When you are ready, lie down and allow yourself to drift into sleep. Repeat this exercise every night for at least a week.

It will take some time to establish a connection with your twin flame, especially if you are new to dream work. Keep a journal near your bed and write everything you can remember about your dreams as soon as you wake up. It is important to do this as the very first thing, before checking your phone or getting up to relieve yourself, since your dreams fade from memory within moments after you open your eyes. If you are unable to remember any dreams of making contact with your twin flame, don't worry. Your subconscious mind will deliver and receive messages long before your conscious mind knows what has even happened.

Love and Healing Meditation

Love and healing meditation for yourself and your twin flame is one of the simplest ways to extend kindness toward yourselves. For those who are new to spiritual healing and energy work, this is the best place to begin.

Close your eyes and take a few deep breaths, clearing your mind of any distracting thoughts and emotions. Allow the stress and tension of your previous day to fade as you focus on your breathing slowly. When you feel sufficiently calm and focused, you may begin the meditation.

Envision yourself in your mind's eye sitting cross-legged with a straight spine, as you hopefully are seated in your physical body. Visualize your energy flowing smoothly up your spine, starting at your tailbone, or root chakra, and moving up through your head, or crown chakra. Take full, deep breaths as you get your energy flowing smoothly.

When you feel that your energy is flowing smoothly through your body, surround yourself with a soft gold or pink light. Imagine that this is a cloud of perfect self-love and accep-tance, and you are bathing yourself in its warm glow. Allow yourself to feel the love and healing that this gentle cloud of soft gold or pink light has to offer you. Let it fill your heart and radiate its warmth throughout your entire body, free-ing energetic and emotional blockages and helping you to feel whole again. Bask in this feeling of safety and bliss for several minutes.

When you are ready, visualize the form of your twin flame sitting cross-legged in front of you. See yourself making and holding eye contact, and imagine that the soft cloud of color begins to extend from your eyes to theirs. As your connection deepens through your extended eye contact, your feeling of love and acceptance also radiates towards your beloved. The cloud of light slowly begins to envelop you both, warming and connecting you to one another. Feel the mutual love that you enjoy together as you enjoy these moments of energetic reunion.

As you feel ready to wrap up the meditation, speak a few words of love to your twin flame. If you feel called to use a term of endearment, such as "my love" or "beloved," feel free to speak freely. You may recall terms of affection that you used with one another from a past life that can help you to awaken your twin. Your message may include senti-ments such as, "I love you so much and cannot wait to meet you," or, "I wish you all the love and healing in the world," or, "I am ready to love and accept you completely."

You can repeat this meditation as often as you like. Enjoy the rejuvenation it brings as you deepen your connection to your twin flame and prepare yourselves to meet in person.

Chapter 4

Using Telepathy to Reach Your Twin Flame

O ne of the most effective ways to pull your twin flame into your life and accelerate your meeting is to reach out to them with telepathy. Because your souls are already one, your ability to communicate with your twin flame via telepathy is enhanced. In fact, you already communicate with one another in this way without even knowing. If you have ever experienced sudden strong thoughts, images, or emotions that seem to come out of nowhere, you may be picking up on the energy of your twin.

Twin flames are never not tuned into one another. By the very nature of their connection, they are always "talking" to one another, sharing experiences, emotions, and wisdom over the chasm of time and space. You may be surprised at how much of your personality and life experiences have been shaped by your connection with your twin flame.

Telepathic communication with your twin flame is so easy, you literally do it in your sleep. Doing it consciously and translating the messages into something you can understand, however, is the tricky part.

What is Telepathy?

Telepathy is a form of communication that happens through the mind. People and animals send a telepathic communication at every moment of every day, storing their thoughts in what is known as the collective unconscious. The collective unconscious is an energetic collection of all thought, emotion, and experience, especially those that are repressed. People share their experiences with one another constantly through accessing the collective unconscious. Simultaneous discoveries or inventions that happen on opposite sides of the world are said to happen because these people accessed similar wavelengths of the collective unconscious.

Telepathy is interpreted by the heart and mind, but it is sent through energetic fields. Each living being is surrounded by an electromagnetic field that extends anywhere from 5 to 15 feet outside of their bodies. This field contains information about our thoughts, feelings, memories, and experiences that can be picked up and interpreted by those with advanced psychic abilities, though people in tune with their natural intuition can read it, too. If you've ever had a gut feeling that someone you know was having a bad day even though all outward signs were showing otherwise, you probably picked up on their true feelings through unknowingly reading their energy field.

We filter all the telepathic information we receive through our unconscious minds. Because most people are out of touch with their unconscious, the messages of telepathic communication go largely uninterpreted. The more sensitive people amongst us often receive large amounts of psychic data, but without the training to interpret this information and filter it in a healthy way, they often become overwhelmed by the incoming sensations, mistaking them for their own.

The unconscious communicates with us in subtle ways every day. The information we receive from our own unconscious and that of others most often manifest as unconscious behaviors and reactions. For example, a knee-jerk emotional reaction to someone's words or actions is a manifestation of our own unconscious thoughts and emotions. These are programmed responses that we have developed as a result of our own past experiences of pain or pleasure.

Our unconscious also speaks to us through dreams. The purpose of the unconscious mind is to shield our conscious awareness from information that would hurt us, so these messages are encrypted in the symbols of our dreams. Psychoanalyzing our dreams provides immense insight into our repressed thoughts, emotions, and memories for healing and self-improvement.

Learning to understand the messages and information we receive through telepathy is an advanced psychic technique that anyone can learn. We all have the ability to hone our natural intuition so that we understand the information coming in with our conscious awareness; this skill merely takes dedicated practice to develop. And there is no better person to practice this skill with than the one person you are constantly tuned into your twin flame.

How to Meditate and Open Your Psychic Senses

Meditation

Before one can become proficient at telepathic communication, one needs to know how to truly meditate. Proper meditation goes much farther than simply sitting quietly with your eyes closed. It is much more difficult to meditate correctly than one would think, which is why meditation is at the core of many spiritual practices. Learning to shut off the constant mind chatter that runs in the backgrounds of our minds takes patience and dedicated effort. Once you learn to clear your mind, you will begin to open yourself to outside communication.

To begin meditating, find a quiet spot where you will not be disturbed. Your phone should be off and all distractions cleared from your area.

Sit upright as you first learn to meditate. You can sit cross-legged on the floor, or you can sit in an upright chair if your back needs more support. What's important is that you maintain your alertness throughout your meditation and do not allow yourself to fall asleep.

Close your eyes and begin taking slow, deep breaths. Inhale to the count of seven, hold for a count of four, and exhale to the count of eight. When you inhale, fill your lungs from the diaphragm up so that your belly expands before the top of your chest. Empty the air completely out of your lungs when you exhale so that your abdomen muscles contract from the push. Learning to breathe deeply is a fundamental part of proper meditative practice.

After you have taken about ten deep breaths with the counting, begin to relax your muscles slowly. Start at your toes, releasing all tension and tightness you are holding in your bones and muscles. Move slowly up your feet, to your ankles, your shins, your knees, thighs, pelvis, abs, chest, shoulders, neck, and head. Relax your upper arms, your elbows, your forearms, your wrists, your hands, and your fingers. Relax your lower back, your mid back, and your upper back. Relax your jaw, allowing your tongue to rest gently against the roof of your mouth. Your body should be completely relaxed during proper meditation.

Finally, return your focus to your breathing and continue to take long, deep breaths. Observe any tendency your mind has to wander without judgment or emotion. The goal is to empty your mind of distracting chatter and to maintain your focus on your breathing. Any time you notice your thoughts start-ing to come in, gently release them and guide your attention back to your breath. This process of quieting mind chatter and emptying the mind is the basis of a meditative practice.

Energy Awareness

The next skill you will need to build to develop your tele-pathic abilities is to cultivate energy awareness. Because all communication and movement are forms of energy, you must be able to sense energy and then learn to interpret it.

The best starting point for energy awareness is to learn to recognize your own energy field, for this is how you first interact with and understand the energies around you. To begin, rub your hands together vigorously until you feel them grow warm with heat. After about 20-30 seconds, stop and pull your hands slowly apart until they are just far enough not to touch one another. You will feel a slight tingling in your hands; this is your energy field.

Pull your hands apart a little more until they are about a quarter inch apart. If you still feel your energy, pull them apart to a half inch; if not, move them closer together. Continue pulling your hands apart until you can no longer feel your energy, bringing them closer until you find it again. If you need to rub your hands together once more, you can. Advanced energy practitioners can feel their energy when their hands are a foot or two apart, and they can bend and shape it for healing.

When you have gained a fair bit of practice with this exercise, try sensing your energy field with other parts of your body. It is usually easiest, to begin with your forearm. Pull your awareness to the skin on your forearm, focusing on every physical detail you can muster. You should be able to gauge the temperature in the room and any slight movements in the air. When you have become fully aware of the surface of your skin, pull your attention to the space a quarter of an inch above your forearm. Do you feel the slight tingle? That is your energy field.

As with the hand exercise, continue pulling your awareness out and in as you find your energy field. Remember, your energy field extends beyond your physical body an average of ten feet, so you can pull out quite far before you lose your field. Repeat this exercise with other parts of your body until you have full awareness of your energy field.

Reading the Energy of Your Surroundings

Once you have cultivated an awareness of your own energy, the next step up is to develop an awareness of the energy around you. Learning to read the energy in your immediate environment is a good starting point because you will be able to practice picking up information coming from outside of yourself without running the risk of confusing the energy and emotions of other people with your own.

For this exercise, take yourself to several different locations outside of your home. Then, simply feel. Feel the air of the place, any smells you pick up, the sights, sounds, and most importantly, the energy. Do any random thoughts or emotions come to you as you try to sense the energy? Do you get any flashes of people who once inhabited or walked through this place? Write down your observations, then go home and research the places you visited to match the histories with what you felt.

Practicing Telepathy with a Partner

Once you have mastered the art of reading the energy of your surroundings, you will be ready to move on to practicing with a partner. There are plenty of different exercises that you can practice with an open-minded companion. A good psychic development book or DVD will give you more ideas, but for now, we'll only focus on a few exercises.

The first exercise is to pick up on the emotions of your partner. Get into a quiet, meditative state while facing your partner. As you do this, ask your partner to focus on a specific memory that is attached to strong emotions for them. They should relive the memory and bring as many of those old feelings to the surface as possible. When you are ready, take their hand and do your best to read their emotions through their energy. Mention any thoughts, feelings, or images that come to your mind as you do this. Do not hold anything back for fear of being wrong, because doubt will cut off the flow of incoming energy. Say whatever you think of; you will learn to sort correct information from incorrect information later.

Another simple exercise is to have your partner bring an item that has significant meaning to them. This should be something small enough to fit in your hands. Repeat the steps of the exercise above, first getting into a meditative state, then tuning into the energy of the item in your hand. Say any thoughts, feelings, or images that come to your mind as they arise. When you are finished, have your partner tell you about the object you are holding so you can compare their account with what you sensed.

You can also do a variation of this exercise with a photo. Your partner should bring a photo of someone you have never met or seen before. Repeat the steps above, telling your partner everything you sense about the nature of their relationship, this person's history, etc.

These psychic development exercises will help you cultivate your telepathic skills. From here, you will be perfectly equipped to begin communicating telepathically with your twin flame.

Find Your Psychic Strengths

As you work on your psychic development, you will find that one means of receiving information is naturally stronger than the others. Each of our physical senses has an energetic equivalent. Our psychic senses are usually strongest in the area of our greatest physical senses. Once you find the area of psychic development that you are most proficient in, you can work on fine-tuning that particular skill.

Dreams

If you have vivid dreams that you remember well upon waking, you may receive your best psychic information through dreams. Work on learning to lucid dream and develop your ability to interpret the symbols and messages of your subconscious mind to master this skill.

Psychic Sight

Visual people often find that their greatest psychic strength is their psychic sight. If this is you, you will likely gain information best through visions or images that come to your mind. You can develop this skill with visual exercises, such as recalling a painting from memory, fully recreating the image of a piece of fruit, and psychic card games with a partner.

Psychic Hearing

If you are an auditory person, listening to lots of music or preferring to listen to audio books rather than read, your psychic hearing may be your strongest area. You will "hear" voices, words, names, directions, and so on in your mind or with your physical ears. Trust these impressions as psychic guidance. You can develop this skill by clearing your mind and writing down whatever words or phrases pop up in your head.

Psychic Touch

People with highly sensitive bodies may find their strengths in psychic touch. If this is you, you'll likely find the best information when you are physically near a person or place so you can better pick up on their energy. You may also feel brushes of energy against yours, experiencing them as breezes, temperature changes, or physical sensations such as touch. Your body might try to move you in certain directions with a pulling or pushing sensation to guide you to where you need to go. To develop this skill, continue working on sensing your energy field and expanding out to sense the energies of other people and objects.

Divination Tools

Some people intuit the best information through using divination tools, such as tarot or oracle cards, runes, scrying (gazing into a pool of water or crystal ball), reading tea leaves, etc. If you are a visual person who can inter-pret symbols well, this may be a good route for you to take. To develop this skill, experiment with different divination tools until you find the one that works best for you. Read books or watch videos that focus on your chosen tool to learn how to gain the best information from it.

Divination tools are one of the best ways to intuit informa-tion about your twin flame because you are able to look at something outside of yourself. This will help you learn to trust your intuition without dismissing it as "just being in your head."

Telepathic Exercises for Finding Your Twin Flame

Here's where things get really exciting! The following are some telepathic exercises you can use to find and commu-nicate with your twin flame after you have practiced several of the basic psychic development exercises above.

Map Exercise

For this exercise, you will need a basic map of the world. Sit somewhere quiet and get yourself into a meditative state. As your mind becomes still, set the intention to connect with your twin flame. As you establish the energetic con-nection, ask your twin where in the world they are. When you are ready, open your eyes and look at the map.

When you feel drawn to a particular region of the map, make a note of the region or country. From here, you can look at a map of the area you were drawn to and repeat the exercise until you find a city, neighborhood, etc. After you meet your twin flame, you can ask if they have ever lived in or visited the areas you felt most drawn to.

If you feel very strongly called to a city or region, try researching that area. If visions or emotions arise as you do this research, it might be a good indication that your twin is there. Alternatively, it could be a place your twin flame is longing to visit, or it could be the location of a past life that either your twin lived or the two of you lived together. You'll have to continue working with your intuition to decipher the precise meaning of the location you received.

Timeline Exercise

For this exercise, you will need to draw out several timelines on different pieces of paper. The first will be in years, beginning at one year and working up to twenty or thirty years. The second timeline will be in months, listing each along the line. The third timeline will be days, marking out each up to 31.

Repeat the steps above to get into a meditative state and connect with your twin flame's energy. Once you have established the connection, visualize your first meeting, pulling in as many details about your twin and the environment as you can. When you are fully connected with this moment, ask your twin when you will meet them.

Open your eyes and look at the year timeline. Your focus will be drawn to one part of the timeline. If you get an exact number, great, but if not, continue narrowing in until you have the correct number. Whichever number gives you the strongest feelings is the correct one.

From there, look at the months. You will feel more strongly pulled to one month than the others, or perhaps to a specific season, where you can narrow the exact time from there. When you are ready, proceed to the days and repeat all the steps until you have an exact date written down.

Be sure to repeat this exercise and the map exercise every month or two as you move forward. The future is not set in stone, and your circumstances will change as you and your twin change. Be patient and make adjustments as necessary. All will unfold in perfect divine timing.

Reading Your Twin Flame's Energy

In a previous chapter, we experimented with receiving information about our twin flames through connecting with their chakras. In this exercise, you will connect with their energy more directly to pick up information about their moods, personality traits, personal history, jobs, likes and dislikes, thoughts, personal appearance, cultural background, and so on.

Get into a meditative state and connect with your twin's energy as above. For this exercise, you must practice the skill of being receptive. Telepathy works both ways: there are a receiver and a transmitter. Most people are naturally more adept at one than the other. However, a well-rounded psychic student will practice cultivating both skills.

Open your energy to your twin flame and then wait. Write down any information that comes to you. Don't try to interpret it as it comes in; simply document everything you see and feel. When you are finished, you can look at your notes and try to make sense of what you found. After doing this exercise several times, you can begin to piece together the information to read patterns, filter out distractions, and build an understanding of this person through your psychic intuition.

Sending a Message to Your Twin Flame

In this exercise, you will practice being the transmitter of telepathic communication. Work yourself into a meditative state and connect with your twin flame's energy in the steps outlined above. When the connection is established, you can begin transmitting your message.

As you work on this exercise, you'll want to begin with very simple messages. Complex messages will be lost in translation, but simple messages are easier to pick up. Since you can't assume that your twin flame will be working on their ability to receive telepathic communication, the simpler, the better.

Some of the initial messages you might want to send your twin flame will include an introduction with your name, your location, an image of your face, or a word, image, or phrase that holds a lot of significance to you. You should send this message on repeat, as though it were a loop of audio or video that you were transmitting in your mind.

If you are sending something visual, hold the image in your mind and repeat a word or short phrase associated with the image. This should reach your twin flame whether they are more visually or more verbally oriented. If you decide on a verbal message, limit it to only one or two sentences at most. Single words are especially effective. Your sentence may go something like: "My love, it's [your name]. I am ready to see you; please meet me in [your location]."

If your message is clear, your twin flame will receive it on an unconscious level, or perhaps in a dream, if they are especially sensitive. Your message will compel them to journey to your location, to seek out people with your name and appearance, or to find ways to connect with the energy, words, or images that you have transmitted.

To deepen your psychic bond with your twin, get into the habit of talking to them regularly throughout your day. Tell them stories about your work, your friends, or your family. Tell them how you feel, what you're thinking or studying, about your favorite foods, and so on. Talk to them about what kind of relationship you want when you come back together, where you would like to travel or live, whether you want pets or children, dates you'd like to go on, movies you'd like to see together, music you want to share with them, and so on.

This daily communication will help your twin flame get to know you better and tune into your energy to better find you. When you finally meet, your twin will think you are the person of their dreams, rather than realize that they wanted you all along and were simply attuned to your energy to want you as you already are!

Continue to transmit your repeat messages on a loop as you deepen your daily conversation, and be sure to take the time to receive any information that is sent back to you.

Chapter 5

Using Visualization and the Law of Attraction to Pull in Your Twin Flame

A s you put out your psychic energy to pull in your twin flame with telepathy, you can boost your efforts enormously by inviting the universe to lend a hand toward your reunion, as well. Using visualization and the Law of Attraction to bring your twin flame into your life is amongst the most powerful things you can do to accelerate your spiritual growth and find the love you have been looking for.

What is Visualization?

Visualization is a powerful tool for creating the reality you want through focus and imagination. Visualization is so effective that it is practiced by many of the world's most successful people, who credit it with their achievements. People from all walks of life, including athletes, politicians, performers, business people, intellectuals, artists, and more have practiced visualization regularly with amazing results.

Visualization gains its effectiveness from a number of factors. For one thing, it helps you to break down barriers in your mind against experiencing a successful outcome for a given situation. We often refrain from imagining best-case scenarios because we are holding on to some notion of being "practical." While this may spare us from a certain level of disappointment, it also prevents us from daring to dream that what we really want is possible—and, as everyone knows, if you can't dream it, you can't turn it into reality. Visualization breaks down these imposed barriers by forcing us to confront what we really want and the truth that we can turn that desire into reality.

Another reason for the effectiveness of visualization is that it prepares the mind for the desired outcome. Have you ever wished that your crush would notice you, maybe taking the time to glance in your direction or give you a verbal opening, only to completely botch your chances when your dream scenario finally happened? The reason you fumbled was that you weren't truly prepared for the manifestation of your wishes. You were so busy telling yourself it would never happen that you never took the time to really think about what you would do or so in the event that it *did* happen.

A bit of visualization would have helped you with that. By visualizing scenarios, you gain the power to prepare yourself to respond to them appropriately and, as an added bonus, to guide the situation towards the outcome you want. Studies have found that using visualization grooms your brain synapses to create desired scenarios and perform in a predetermined manner. Hence, with visualization, you are literally prepping yourself for the successful outcome of a situation you may never have even believed was possible!

The most effective visualization practices come from fully envisioning as much detail in a situation as possible. The more engaged your senses are, the more realistic your visualization will be, and therefore, the deeper your self-programming will be. When using visualization, you should imagine as many sights, sounds, smells, tastes, and physical sensations as possible.

Another effective aspect of visualization is envisioning alternative versions of your desired scenario and preparing responses to each. Although you are working to create the exact situation that you desire, life doesn't always go exactly as planned. However, you can still create a successful outcome by preparing for other versions of your scenario rather than allow yourself to become blindsided by a sudden twist and losing your ability to respond appropriately.

What is the Law of Attraction?

Visualization works hand in hand with the Law of Attraction. The Law of Attraction is, in essence, the universal tendency of "like attracts like," as first pointed out by the Greek philosopher Plato. This can be interpreted to mean that you pull the things that you think about into your life.

Your perspective plays a big part in this.

If you have a negative outlook on life, you will create more negative situations ahead of you. You'll even see positive situations in a negative light if your negative habits are deeply ingrained enough. On the other hand, if you have a positive outlook on life, you'll create more positivity in your life, likely because you can turn even the dreariest of situations into reasons to be grateful.

The Law of Attraction goes beyond the powers of perspective into a cosmic theory of how a certain type of energy will attract other energies on similar wavelengths. This is the foundation of the theory of energy vibration: all matter and energy vibrate at the atomic level. The faster the rate of vibration, the lighter the mass of the object is. Spiritual energy vibrates at a very high vibration, so as you become more spiritual, your frequency increases. As a result, you will cosmically attract other people, objects, places, and situations that resonate with your higher vibration and mirror your spiritual energy.

Where visualization pairs with the Law of Attraction are that your repetitive thoughts will access the energy of a given situation (the people, places, and things involved in this situation) and "attract" it to you. You will actually manipulate the energy around you to flow in the direction of your thoughts. This is something we all do every day anyway, but working with the Law of Attraction directly means that you do this consciously and with specific intentions about the people, places, things, and situations you wish to pull into your life. Hence, if you focus your thoughts and intentions on finding and meeting your twin flame, you involve the energy of the universe in your mission (which is already rooting for you anyway) and boost your chances of getting what you want exponentially.

Visualization & Law of Attraction Exercises

With these challenges, you will be working at a higher level of energy manipulation than you ever have before. Here you will combine both the Law of Attraction and the method of visualization to "see" your twin flame, to create your meeting, and to guide your paths to cross in the best possible timing and energy for you both.

Highway Intersection Exercise

For this exercise, you will want to follow the steps to get into a meditative state and connect with your twin flame's energy as detailed in Chapter 4. When you are ready, you can begin the visualization.

With your eyes closed, envision yourself driving along a two-lane country highway in your car. You are driving at a relatively fast speed, soaking in the scenery of the countryside. As you do this, you feel completely happy and completely at peace with where you are in your journey, and you take the time to soak in as many of the details around you as you can. You feel the texture of the steering wheel between your hands, the texture of the seat supporting you, the temperature of the air in your car, the breeze blowing through your hair from your cracked windows. Everything feels perfect.

You're driving along listening to your favorite song, perhaps singing along. A wild exhilaration pulses through your body. You know that something amazing will happen today. You continue to soak in all the sights and sounds along your drive, smelling sweet, fragrant flowers as you pass a well-tended garden. You can taste the coffee or tea in your cup, and you continue to sip merely to enjoy the delicious flavor. All your senses are stimulated with pleasure. You couldn't imagine a more perfect day.

Up ahead, you see a sign indicating that you will come to a four-way stop. You ease your car to a gentle stop, noticing another car pulling up to the intersection directly across from you. As you gaze through the windshield, you meet the eyes of your twin flame, who notices and recognizes you at the exact moment that you see and recognize them. Spend the next several minutes imagining what comes next.

Energetic Cords Exercise

As you sit in a quiet place, work yourself into a meditative state and connect with the energy of your twin flame. When the connection is established, you can begin the exercise.

With your eyes closed, tune yourself into an awareness of your energy field. As you find the edges of your energy, see your energy "bubble" filled with a vibrant hue of your favorite color. This cloud of color radiates peace and happiness throughout your entire being. You could hardly imagine feeling better than you do at this moment.

In your bliss, you look down and see a silky white cord extending from your heart. As you gaze lovingly down at this natural cord, you realize that this is the bond of energy that connects you to your twin flame. The cord extends from you into a cloud of ether, and though you cannot see the end, you know that your beloved is on the other side.

Gently, you take the cord in your fingers and pluck it slightly. As the cord vibrates from the motion, you know that it contains a question to your twin flame: Are you ready to reunite? When the cord grows still, you wait for a response. After a few moments the cord begins to vibrate again, and you know you have received your answer: yes.

You reach your hands up and wrap them around the cord. Despite its delicate appearance, you find that this cord is unbelievably strong. Nothing could break it; it is your eternal bond. You eagerly but gently begin to pull on the cord, drawing your beloved closer to you on the other end. You feel the cord go taught, knowing that your twin is pulling, as well. You continue to pull until the vast expanse of space has closed between you. Before you know it, you are gazing into the eyes of your twin flame, radiating warmth and love to one another in this ethereal place. Spend the next few minutes imagining what will happen next.

Visualizing Your Twin Flame Exercise

In this exercise, you will draw on your psychic development practice from the previous chapters to receive information about your twin flame as you use visualization to bring your intuitive insight to life.

As you sit in a quiet place, work yourself into a meditative state and connect with the energy of your twin flame. When the connection is established, you may begin the exercise.

Close your eyes and visualize yourself sitting cross-legged, your spine perfectly erect. Seated directly across from you, so close your knees are almost touching, is your twin flame. Your heart pounds with excitement as you feel yourself in the energy of your beloved, and you feel the intense love that already exists between you.

The first thing you notice is how overwhelmingly attracted you are to your twin. Everything about their appearance overwhelms your senses with pleasure. Notice the details of their clothes, their style, their mood, their personality. Open your intuition to receive information as you proceed so that you are not projecting your preconceived notions onto the person before you.

As you continue to receive details about your twin flame, do your best to visualize them. Notice the shape of the face, the skin tone, the color and style of the hair, the color and shape of the eyes, the body build, the posture, the facial expression. What does their appearance tell you about them? What can you read off their energy about what type of person they are?

Engage the rest of your senses in your visualization. What does your twin flame smell like? Do they wear any perfume or cologne? Imagine that your twin suddenly speaks, perhaps saying their name and greeting you. What does their voice sound like? Do they sound kind, commanding, nervous, playful?

Now it is time to interact with your twin flame. Visualize yourself extending your hand in greeting. Your twin flame takes your hand, and you feel your energies meet for the first time. How does their skin feel? Is the hand small or large? From the hand, your fingers move to their face, exploring the lines of their jaw, the skin of their cheek, the hair at their temples. Finally, you pull in closer for a kiss. How do your beloved's lips feel beneath yours? How do they taste and smell? Feel the electric pleasure wash over you as your kiss deepens and you give in to the passion between you. Spend a few minutes imagining what happens next.

Meeting Your Twin Flame Exercise

This exercise will challenge you to fully create and direct a real-life scenario that will likely come true. You will need to be intensely focused and intentional to bring it properly to life. It helps to have an idea of what your ideal scenario will be before you begin the exercise. Do you wish to have your twin find you? Would you prefer to go out into the world and find your twin? Would you meet somewhere you are both traveling to for the first time?

When you have your dream scenario mapped out in your head, sit in a quiet place to work yourself into a meditative state and connect with the energy of your twin flame. Once the connection is established, you can begin the exercise.

Play through the scenario you planned in your mind. Pay careful attention to the details in your visualization, bringing it perfectly to life in your head. What do you see/hear/

smell/taste/feel? What does your twin say to you? Who speaks first? How does your initial interaction go? What is their attitude? Is the interaction playful, flirty, intense, or romantic? Remember to play for the moment that your eyes first meet, and the feeling this gives you both. The moment of recognition is the most important in your meeting.

As you go through your visualization, be sure to include alternate versions of the meeting. What would you do if you recognized your twin flame, but they didn't recognize you? What if they did recognize you, but were overwhelmed or frightened? What if you recognized them at a distance, but had too many obstacles between you? What if the initial reaction of your twin was unpleasant? What if you say something awkward? Take the time to work through every possibility you can imagine and your responses to each. Every scenario should have a successful outcome, even if it takes time and a fair bit of creativity to bring it about.

The key to all these exercises is repetition. With this exercise, in particular, you will walk through a number of scenarios, but the one you will repeat most is your ideal scenario. Pour most of your energy into creating a perfect meeting, where you run into one another in a comfortable manner, and both respond favorably to the exchange.

Chapter 6

Magick and Daily Rituals for Finding Your Twin Flame

The tools and practices available to you to help you find and meet your twin flame are many and varied, but the most effective means of creation is daily practice. In this chapter, we will explore avenues of manifestation that include more formal ritual and a dedicated spiritual practice as a means of meeting one's twin flame. These practices also draw upon the principles of visualization, telepathy, and the Law of Attraction for their power and effectiveness, so the learning we have gained so far will build upon itself with these new tools.

What is Magick?

Magick is synonymous with the universal forces of fate, destiny, coincidence, synchronicity, and alignment. Magick is the power that moves significant people into our lives, opens the doors of opportunity, brings abundance and good fortune to us, and puts us in the right place at the right time for fate to have its way with us. Magick is the place where the sacred meets the mundane and where the ordinary meets the supernatural. At its heart, magick is the source of all beauty and wonder in the world.

Magick practitioners, who often go by names such as "witch" or "wizard," use formalized rituals to focus their intentions and aid them in channeling the energy of magick towards manifesting their wishes and goals. This type of work is often called "spellwork," which is another word for ritual.

Spells are different from other visualization and Law of Attraction practices in that they use physical tools and actions to seal the intention of one's energy work. Although spells also operate under the principles of visualization and the Law of Attraction, they go one step beyond these meditation exercises by following through with a physical action. Spellwork also comes in tandem with unique religious or cultural belief systems and practices and is practiced in a variety of different cultures.

Love Spells

For this ritual, we will stick with a basic candle magick love spell, which anyone can practice. Those who wish to find more elaborate spells can find them in dedicated spell books, which also provide more advanced training and considerations.

You will need:

- A red or pink candle

- A flame-proof candle holder
- A carving tool, such as a knife or needle
- Rose essential oil
- A book of runes and symbols
- Pen and paper

To begin, use the pen and paper to write down your intentions for the spell. It is best to set your intention to attract your twin flame rather than try to attract a specific person. This openness will allow the universe to find the best way to manifest your desires rather than trying to force a specific person or personality to conform to your wishes. For instance, if you know the identity of your twin flame, invoke them as your twin flame rather than as the person they are in this lifetime. This will call on their higher self, who will push beyond the fears and limitations of the current ego identity of your beloved.

Refer to your book of runes to find symbols that match your intentions. Hearts and runes that symbolize love, marriage, strengthening of bonds, and completion of goals are all appropriate symbols for this spell.

Take your knife or needle and carve your selected runes into the wax of your candle. Hold the candle in both hands, focusing on visualizing your relationship you're your twin flame. Imagine your meeting, the bliss of the honeymoon phase, and the two of you living together harmoniously. Draw upon your practice with visualization to bring your visions to life in your mind's eye.

Charge the candle with your intentions of finding and re-uniting with your twin flame. Feel the energy of your intense desire pour into the wax of the candle, burying itself in its core. When you are finished, anoint your candle with the rose oil by rubbing it over the entire surface, except for the wick.

Place the candle in its holder and light the wick. Gaze into the flame as the candle burns, visualizing the manifestation of your intentions. As you watch the candle burn, repeat the following intentions to yourself: "The flame of this candle burns like the passion of my love for my twin flame. I see our flames united as one. As the candle burns, the energy of my intentions is released into the universe to manifest in reality."

Allow the candle to burn to completion. If you must extinguish the flame before it burns down, snuff the flame rather than blowing it out. This will preserve the energy of your spell for when you return to burn it down.

Write a Letter to Your Twin Flame

This exercise is very straightforward: write a letter to your twin flame. Unlike the telepathic transmission exercise, where you needed to keep your message simple, this exercise gives you the freedom to say anything and everything you want.

When you are finished, you may hold the letter over a flame to burn it. As you do, imagine that the smoke is carrying your message to your lover on the wind. Collect the ashes and release them into a strong breeze, or drop them into a moving body of water, such as a river, stream, or the ocean, visualizing the water or breeze carrying your message to your twin flame wherever they are in the world.

Daily Habits for Finding Your Twin

For the best results in your quest to find and reunite with your twin flame, you will want to develop daily habits to draw them into your life. Our habits form the basis of our lives. Good habits will keep our lives running smoothly, while bad habits will put a barrage of obstacles in our way. Creating a daily habit of attracting your twin will help you to integrate them into your life before you ever even meet, which is one of the most powerful uses of the Law of Attraction you can find.

Daily Prayer

If prayer appeals to you, write a daily prayer for finding your twin flame. Invoke whichever deity or form of universal energy appeals to you most. Be specific with your prayer.

Daily Meditation

This is great for simply "spending time" with your twin flame. Clear your mind and connect with your twin, then just enjoy the feeling of the connection.

Daily Visualization

Make one of the visualization exercises from Chapter 5 a daily practice. Better yet, invent your own visualization exercise!

Daily Communication

As we saw in the chapter on telepathy, "talking to" your twin flame throughout your day will strengthen your bond and help them bring you more fully into your life. For bonus points, talk to them before bed as you would your lover, imagining them lying in bed next to you discussing your days at work and other obligations.

Daily Affirmations

Affirmations are the practice of repeating a phrase or mantra to yourself to provide encouragement and positive reinforcement as you work towards a specific goal. These repeated words also draw on the Law of Attraction for their power, especially when we repeat affirmations that invoke a reality where our dreams are already manifest. Some powerful twin flame affirmations include:

- I feel my twin flame moving closer to me every day.
- My bond with my twin flame is closer than ever.
- I see my twin flame fully embedded in my life.
- I will do whatever it takes to find my twin flame.
- My twin flame and I are perfectly happy and perfectly in love.
- I am so pleased that I have finally met my twin flame.

Be sure to write your own affirmations as they come to you. The more personal your mantras, the more effective they will be.

Use your creativity to find ways to pull your twin flame into your life more and more every day. The greater your practice, the quicker you will find them, and the more time you will have to spend together, basking in your love and passion for one another.

Chapter 7

Preparing Yourself to Meet Your Twin Flame

With all you have learned in the previous pages, your meeting with your twin flame is sure to happen much sooner than it would have otherwise. However, this work would not be well done unless you take the time to prepare yourself for the realization of your dreams. How can you tell whether your efforts are working—and more importantly, what do you do when you succeed?

How to Recognize When Your Twin is Near

The time leading up to the fateful meeting will be marked by vivid dreams of your twin. Though you may not know what he or she looks like, you will still sense this person's essence, knowing the relationship that this person has with you. Pay attention to the details and conversations in these dreams, for they may hold clues about when and how to find your twin.

You will also notice a strong sense of fate or destiny. This can manifest as anticipation, nervousness, exhilaration, or restlessness. Signs and synchronicities will put themselves in your path to alert you that the time to meet your twin flame is drawing near. Be on the lookout for recurring numbers, words, names, patterns, encounters with animals, and so on to clue you in to what's happening.

Following Your Intuition

You may also find yourself feeling sudden impulses to go to specific places, or to try new things. Perhaps you will be drawn to drop everything and go somewhere immediately, either somewhere you know of or just on an aimless walk. You may also feel the urge to talk to strangers or to call a friend and see what they're doing for the evening.

These impulses can be signs from your intuition that you are on course to meet your twin flame. Follow your intuition and allow yourself to indulge these impulses. They will likely lead you to the moment of your meeting with your beloved.

What to Expect When You First See Your Twin

To those who know what to look for, the initial meeting with your twin flame is powerful and distinct. When your eyes first meet, you will feel it like an energetic punch to the gut or an electric shiver down your spine. The moment will be forever imprinted in your mind's eye, and you will have a feeling that this moment has happened before. A profound sense of recognition will also accompany this initial eye contact. You will feel simultaneously shaken and at ease, and your body may take a while to balance these conflicting impulses.

After you part ways, you will find yourself missing your twin flame within moments of your separation. It may seem strange to miss someone you just met so intensely. This is yet another sign that you have just encountered your twin.

I Met My Twin...So Now What?

Ideally, this initial meeting will have opened the door to future meetings. If possible, be sure to exchange numbers or to connect on social media. You might also try to discover whether your twin flame is likely to return to the location of your meeting, or whether they go somewhere nearby regularly where you can meet up again, such as a local coffee shop or yoga class. At the very least, be sure to get their name, both first and last, either by exchanging business cards or asking outright.

Be prepared to go through all the stages of the twin flame reunion as your relationship progresses. While you can certainly hope for smooth sailing, you will encounter some difficulties. Remember, the purpose of the twin flame connection is to test and challenge you to grow. You *will* face obstacles and difficulties, but with the right amount of love and effort, you can overcome them. Such is your destiny, after all.

Every love story is unique and complete unto itself. This is your love story, and in these moments, you have the power to author it as you choose. As long as you are open to allowing parts of the story to write themselves, and you have the resolve to navigate all waters that lie ahead, the love story of you and your twin flame will be everything you need and so much more.

Conclusion

Thank you, dear reader, for sticking through to the end! There are so many resources available on twin flames and soulmates, and I am truly honored that you chose mine. I hope that this work brings you healing and love beyond your wildest dreams. Your dedication to finding your twin shows that you deserve it.

As you work with these exercises in the days, weeks, and months to come, you will find that you naturally adapt them to fit your needs and intentions. Please feel free to do this as you feel called to. The more personal your practice, the more effective it will ultimately prove to be.

You will likely also find yourself more drawn to one method of attracting your twin flame than the others. People with strong psychic potential will gravitate towards telepathic communication while those with strong creative streaks and powerful imaginations will find the most value in the visualization exercises. Those with a strong draw to organized and formal ritual practice may feel called to learn more about magick and spellwork, while natural healers will find themselves repeating the love and healing meditations.

There is no wrong path to finding your beloved. The way back into one another's arms has already been determined, long before you ever set foot on this Earth. Though the details can and will change as you both grow and evolve, the major lessons and growth will remain the same. Above all, remember to be patient, to be flexible, to enjoy the journey, and to trust in the strength of your bond and the perfect, divine timing of this wondrous and abundant universe.

Thank you again, and I wish you all the love and happiness in the world.